AN INTRODUCTION TO

FROGS

BY MICHAEL TYLER

DESIGNED BY LYNN TWELFTREE

BOOKSHELF

Stanley Thornes

Published by

Multimedia International (UK) Ltd

by arrangement with

Horwitz Grahame Pty Ltd

Exclusively distributed
in the United Kingdom,
Eire and Europe by:

Stanley Thornes (Publishers) Ltd
Old Station Drive
Leckhampton
Cheltenham
GL53 0DN
England

Copyright © 1989 text: Michael Tyler

ISBN 0 7487 0013 7
Series ISBN (Stage 4) 0 7487 0023 4

Printed and bound in Hong Kong
by Dai Nippon (HK) Ltd

1 2 3 4 5 6 7 8 9 10 11 12
89 90 91 92 93

Acknowledgements

Cover photograph and photograph page 6 by Margaret
Davies
Photographs pages 4, 10, 11 (bottom right) & 15 by
Heather Angel
Photograph page 26 by Dale Caville
Photographs pages 7, 9 (top), 11 (top), 12, 14
(right), 16 (right), 19, 23 & 24 by Densey Clyne
Photographs pages 11 (bottom left) & 20 by Jim Frazier
Photographs pages 14 (left), 16 (left) & 18 by Murray
Littlejohn
Photograph page 25 by Fred Parker
Photograph page 13 by Bohdan
Stankewytsch-Janusch
Photographs of burrowing sequence, pages 8-9,
reproduced by kind permission of the Queensland
Museum
Diagrams by Lynn Twelftree

The publishers would like to thank Densey Clyne, Mantis
Wildlife, for her assistance.

Contents

Types of frogs

So far 4000 different species of frog have been found in the world and scientists believe that others will be discovered. There are six different species of frogs (including two species of toad) in Great Britain. One of these, the agile frog, is only found in the Channel Islands.

Scientists divide frogs into a number of groups called families. The frogs are grouped according to the way they look and the way they live.

Tree frogs are found in many countries and belong to one family. They usually live in trees and bushes. They have sticky discs on the tips of their fingers and toes to help them climb on smooth leaves and branches. There are no tree frogs in Great Britain.

Types of frogs

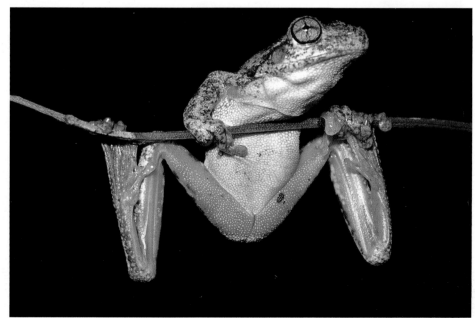

Land and water frogs are found worldwide, and belong to many different families. These frogs are found in all kinds of places, including rainforests and deserts. They live in the water, or on the ground, or in burrows.

Many of the desert frogs burrow with the help of a spade-like projection on each foot.

Sequence of photographs showing desert frog burrowing

Rainforest frog (left)

Features of frogs

Frogs vary in size. The largest frog in the world, *Conraua goliath* in West Africa, is about 300mm long; and the smallest frog in the world, *Sminthillus limbatus* in Cuba, is 12mm. The largest frog in Great Britain, the marsh frog, is 125mm long; and the smallest, called the edible frog, is only 60mm long.

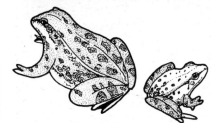

The smallest frog in Great Britain (above)

The largest frog in Great Britain (right)

Scale drawing showing difference in size between these two species (left)

All frogs are similar in important ways.

They have smooth skin which must be kept moist. For this reason they always live in or near damp places.

Desert habitat where frogs keep moist by living underground until it rains (right)

Tropical habitat with natural springs where tree, land and water frogs live (bottom left)

Village pond, typical habitat of frogs in Great Britain (bottom right)

Frogs' eyes and nostrils are on top of their heads so that they are able to see and breathe while the rest of the body is under water.

Most frogs are excellent swimmers. Some kick with their strong back legs but others use a dog-paddle style.

Features of frogs

Frogs have short arms and long legs to help them leap. A species of frog in South Africa holds the world record for leaping: 10.3 metres in three leaps.

The rocket frog is found in eastern and northern Australia. It is known to jump long distances

Most frogs are green or brown and are hard to see. The Australian corroboree frog, with its bright colours, seems to stand out but it also blends in with its surroundings.

A common brown frog (above)

Australian corroboree frog (right)

Features of frogs

Frogs and toads

Toads have warty skin, stout bodies and short legs, and crawl and hop rather than leap. Two species of toads, the common toad and the natterjack toad, are found in Great Britain. Toads are often poisonous.

Natterjack toad

Frog calls

Frogs make a variety of calls for different reasons. During breeding time the male makes a call to attract females. This call also tells other males that the territory is now occupied. Each species of frog has its own call and to make the sound louder the male blows up his throat. Male and female frogs also give a high-pitched scream or a series of chirrups if they are distressed, and a grunt or squawk as a warning sound.

The life cycle of frogs

The life cycle of frogs and the development of the young varies from one species to another. The following describes the life cycle of one common frog.

During breeding time, the male frog goes to the breeding place and calls mostly at night.

The female comes to the breeding place and lays many eggs. This may take several hours. While laying the eggs she raises her hands just above the surface of the water and throws them down, creating air bubbles. Behind her the male pours his fertilising fluid over the eggs. Frogs' eggs are coated with a jelly which protects them. We call groups of frogs' eggs frog spawn. Some British frogs lay about 10,000 eggs at a time while others lay only 1000.

The life cycle of frogs

Marsh frogs laying and fertilising eggs (left)

Marsh frog spawn (above)

The eggs slowly develop into tadpoles over a period of a few days. When the tadpoles are ready to escape from the jelly they wriggle and break out through the jelly wall.

While they are growing, tadpoles spend all of their time feeding. At this stage of development they have many rows of teeth, which they use to scrape food from stems and rocks or from the bottom of the pond. Later they may feed on insects and other small creatures in the water.

Inside a tadpole's mouth

teeth

horny beak

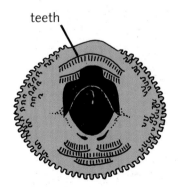

Peron's tree frog tadpole

giant burrowing frog tadpole

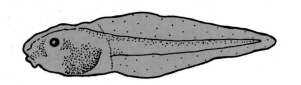

After several weeks legs grow outside the tadpoles' bodies. Arms grow under the skin and then break through the skin when they are fully developed.

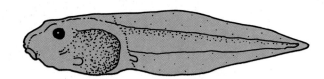

Development of a tadpole (left)

Tadpole with legs developed (opposite)

When tadpoles are ready to leave the water their tails become smaller and smaller as they are absorbed into the body. In one or two days nothing is left of the tail. Lungs have developed and the tadpoles have now become frogs.

The life cycle of frogs

Some frogs do not lay their eggs in water. They lay them in little nests on moist ground so that the eggs do not dry out and there is enough water for the tadpoles to begin to grow in their jelly capsules. When heavy rain falls the tadpoles are washed into a pond where they complete their growth.

The life cycle of frogs

The tadpoles of some species stay inside their capsules until they reach the frog stage. The eggs of these species need to be laid on very moist ground and the capsules need to be strong to withstand the kicking of the babies as they grow.

Developing tadpole shown without its protective capsule

The stomach brooding frog has a most unusual life cycle. The female swallows her eggs or young tadpoles and keeps them in her stomach. The tadpoles produce a chemical to stop the stomach from making acid so that they are not digested. When the tadpoles have developed into little frogs they are born through the mother's mouth.

How tadpoles and frogs breathe

When frogs are at the tadpole stage they can breathe under water because they have gills. Adult frogs breathe with lungs, as humans do, but they also breathe through their skin, getting oxygen from the air or water. To be able to breathe through their skin frogs must keep the skin moist. They also breathe through the roofs of their mouths.

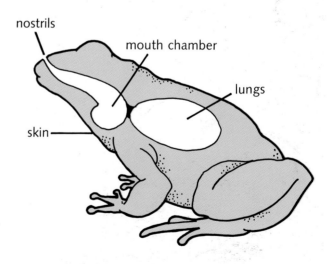

nostrils

mouth chamber

lungs

skin

What frogs eat

Frogs eat insects, snails and other small creatures including other frogs! To catch insects they flick out their long, sticky tongues on to their prey. They then flick their tongues back into their mouths. The food is not chewed even though some frogs have teeth.

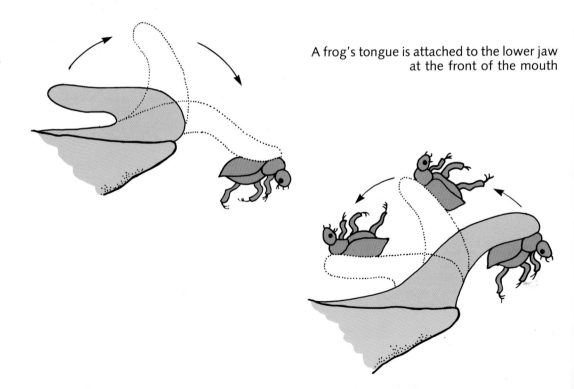

A frog's tongue is attached to the lower jaw at the front of the mouth

Caring
for
tadpoles

The time to collect eggs in Great Britain is from December to April, and tadpoles from February to May.

A good home for tadpoles is a large bowl, a plastic bucket, or (best of all) a glass aquarium.

It is best to use water from the pond where you have collected the eggs or tadpoles. Tap water contains chlorine which kills tadpoles. To rid tap water of chlorine, let it stand in a bucket for 24 hours before using it.
Keep only a few tadpoles in one container.

The best food for tadpoles is lettuce leaves which have been boiled until they are limp; or dried, tropical fish food. Make sure there is always just enough food in the aquarium and that you cover the top of the container with wire or cloth so that the froglets do not jump out. Without water, the froglets cannot survive.

When their arms are starting to appear provide a raft or bench on to which the froglets can climb or rest.

Return the baby frogs to their original environment.

Index

Frogs depicted in this book

Habitats depicted in this book